PLANT BASED DIET COOKBOOK

SIDE DISH RECIPES

Quick, Easy and Delicious Recipes
for a lifelong Health

Amanda Grant

Legal Disclaimer

The information contained in this book and its contents is not designed to replace any form of medical or professional advice; and is not meant to replace the need for independent medical, financial, legal, or other professional advice or service that may require. The content and information in this book have been provided for educational and entertainment purposes only.

The content and information contained in this book have been compiled from sources deemed reliable, and they are accurate to the best of the Author's knowledge, information and belief. However, the Author cannot guarantee its accuracy and validity and therefore cannot be held liable for any errors and/or omissions.

Further, changes are periodically made to this book as needed. Where appropriate and/or necessary, you must consult a professional (including but not limited to your doctor, attorney, financial advisor, or other such professional) before using any of the suggested remedies, techniques, and/or information in this book.

Upon using this book's contents and information, you agree to hold harmless the Author from any damaged, costs and expenses, including any legal fees potentially resulting from the application of any of the information in this book. This disclaimer applies to any loss, damages, or injury caused by the use and application of this book's content, whether directly and indirectly, whether for breach of contract, tort, negligence, personal injury, criminal intent, or under any other circumstances.

You agree to accept all risks of using the information presented in this book. You agree that by continuing to read this book, where appropriate and/or necessary, you shall consult a professional (including but not limited to your doctor, attorney, financial advisor, or other such professional) before remedies, techniques, and/or information in this book.

<u>*TABLE OF CONTENTS*</u>

Side Dishes RECIPES

Thai Snack Mix

Servings: 4

Cooking Time: 90 Minutes

Ingredients:

- 5 cups mixed nuts
- 1 cup chopped dried pineapple
- 1 cup pumpkin seed
- 1 teaspoon onion powder
- 1 teaspoon garlic powder
- 2 teaspoons paprika
- 1/2 teaspoon ground black pepper
- 1 teaspoon of sea salt
- 1/4 cup coconut sugar
- 1/2 teaspoon red chili powder
- 1 tablespoon red pepper flakes
- 1/2 tablespoon red curry powder
- 2 tablespoons soy sauce
- 2 tablespoons coconut oil

Directions:

- Switch on the slow cooker, add all the ingredients in it except for dried pineapple and red pepper flakes, stir until combined and cook for 90 minutes at high heat setting, stirring every 30 minutes.
- When done, spread the nut mixture on a baking sheet lined with parchment paper and let it cool.
- Then spread dried pineapple on top, sprinkle with red pepper flakes and serve.

Nutrition Info: Calories: 230 Cal ;Fat: 17.5 g :Carbs: 11.5 g ;Protein: 6.5 g ;Fiber: 2 g

Sherry Roasted King Trumpet

Servings: 4

Cooking Time: 20 Minutes

Ingredients:

- 1 ½ pounds king trumpet mushrooms, cleaned and sliced in half lengthwise.
- 2 tablespoons olive oil
- 4 cloves garlic, minced or chopped
- 1/2 teaspoon dried rosemary
- 1/2 teaspoon dried thyme
- 1/2 teaspoon dried parsley flakes
- 1 teaspoon Dijon mustard
- 1/4 cup dry sherry
- Sea salt and freshly ground black pepper, to taste

Directions:

- Start by preheating your oven to 390 degrees F. Line a large baking pan with parchment paper.

1. In a mixing bowl, toss the mushrooms with the remaining ingredients until well coated on all sides.

- Place the mushrooms in a single layer on the prepared baking pan.

2. Roast the mushrooms for approximately 20 minutes, tossing them halfway through the cooking.
3. Bon appétit!

Nutrition Info: Per Serving: Calories: 138; Fat: 7.8g; Carbs: 11.8g; Protein: 5.7g

Hummus Quesadillas

Servings: 1

Cooking Time: 8 Minutes

Ingredients:

- 1 tortilla, whole-grain, about 8-inches
- 1/3 cup hummus, ¼ cup sautéed spinach
- 2 tablespoons chopped sun-dried tomatoes
- 2 tablespoons sliced Kalamata olives
- 1 teaspoon olive oil

Directions:

- Take a tortilla, spread hummus on its one side, then cover its one-half with spinach, tomatoes, and olives and fold it.
- Take a medium skillet pan, place it over medium heat and when hot, place folded quesadilla in it, cook for minutes and then flip it carefully.
- Brush with oil, continue cooking for 2 minutes, flip again and cook for 2 minutes until golden brown.
- When done, transfer quesadilla to a cutting board, slice it into wedges and serve.

Nutrition Info: Calories: 187 Cal ;Fat: 9 g :Carbs: 16.3 g ;Protein: 10.4 g ;Fiber: 0 g

Tomato And Basil Bruschetta

Servings: 12

Cooking Time: 6 Minutes

Ingredients:

- 3 tomatoes, chopped
- ¼ cup chopped fresh basil
- 1 tablespoon extra-virgin olive oil
- pinch of sea salt
- 1 baguette, cut into 12 slices
- 1 garlic clove, sliced in half

Directions:

- Preparing the Ingredients
- In a small bowl, combine the tomatoes, basil, olive oil, and salt and stir to mix. Set aside. Preheat the oven to 4°F.
- Place the baguette slices in a single layer on a baking sheet and toast in the oven until brown for about 6 minutes.
- Finish and Serve
- Flip the bread slices over once during cooking. Remove from the oven and rub the bread on both sides with the sliced clove of garlic.

- Top with the tomato-basil mixture and serve immediately.

Nutrition Info: Calories: 130 Cal ;Fat: 4 g :Carbs: 14.3 g ;Protein: 7.4 g ;Fiber: 0 g

Broccoli And White Beans With Potatoes And Walnuts

Servings: 4

Cooking Time: 35 Minutes

Ingredients:

- 1½ pounds fingerling potatoes
- 4 cups broccoli florets
- 3 tablespoons extra-virgin olive oil
- 3 garlic cloves, minced
- ¾ cup chopped walnut pieces
- ¼ teaspoon crushed red pepper
- 1½ cups or 1 (15.5-ounce) can white beans, drained and rinsed
- 1 teaspoon dried savory
- Salt and freshly ground black pepper
- 1 tablespoon fresh lemon juice

Directions:

- Preparing the Ingredients

1. Steam the potatoes until tender for about minutes. Set aside.
2. Steam the broccoli until crisp-tender. Set aside.

- In a large skillet, heat 2 tablespoons of the oil over medium heat. Add the garlic, walnuts, and crushed red pepper. Cook until the garlic is softened.

3. Stir in the steamed potatoes and broccoli. Add the beans and savory, then season with salt and black pepper. Cook until heated through.
4. Finish and Serve
5. Sprinkle with lemon juice and drizzle with the remaining 1 tablespoon olive oil.
6. Serve immediately.

Nutrition Info: Calories: 177 Cal ;Fat: 7 g :Carbs: 20.3 g ;Protein: 9 g ;Fiber: 0 g

French Haricots Verts

Servings: 4

Cooking Time: 10 Minutes

Ingredients:

- 1 ½ cups vegetable broth
- 1 Roma tomato, pureed
- 1 ½ pounds Haricots Verts, trimmed
- 4 tablespoons olive oil
- 2 garlic cloves, minced
- 1/2 teaspoon red pepper
- 1/2 teaspoon cumin seeds
- 1/2 teaspoon dried oregano
- Sea salt and freshly ground black pepper, to taste
- 1 tablespoon fresh lemon juice

Directions:

- Bring the vegetable broth and pureed tomato to a boil. Add in the Haricots Verts and let it cook for about 5 minutes until Haricots Verts are crisp-tender; reserve.
- In a saucepan, heat the olive oil over medium-high heat; sauté the garlic for 1 minute or until aromatic.

- Add in the spices and reserved green beans; let it cook for about minutes until cooked through.
- Serve with a few drizzles of the fresh lemon juice. Bon appétit!

Nutrition Info: Per Serving: Calories: 197; Fat: 14.5g; Carbs: 14.4g; Protein: 5.4g

Rosemary And Garlic Roasted Carrots

Servings: 4

Cooking Time: 25 Minutes

Ingredients:

- 2 pounds carrots, trimmed and halved lengthwise
- 4 tablespoons olive oil
- 2 tablespoons champagne vinegar
- 4 cloves garlic, minced, 2 sprigs rosemary,
- Sea salt and ground black pepper, to taste
- 4 tablespoons pine nuts, chopped

Directions:

- Begin by preheating your oven to 400 degrees F.
- Toss the carrots with the olive oil, vinegar, garlic, rosemary, salt and black pepper. Arrange them in a single layer on a parchment-lined roasting sheet.
- Roast the carrots in the preheated oven for about 20 minutes, until fork-tender.
- Garnish the carrots with the pine nuts and serve immediately. Bon appétit!

Nutrition Info: Per Serving: Calories: 80; Fat: 8.2g; Carbs: 11.8g; Protein: 1.8g

Sushi-style Quinoa

Servings: 4

Cooking Time: 25 Minutes

Ingredients:

- 2 cups water
- 1 cup dry quinoa, rinsed
- ¼ cup unseasoned rice vinegar
- ¼ cup mirin or white wine vinegar

Directions:

- Preparing the Ingredients.
- In a large saucepan, bring the water to boil. Add the quinoa to the boiling water, stir, cover, and reduce the heat to low. Simmer for 15- minutes, until the liquid is absorbed. Remove from the heat and let it stand for 5 minutes.
- Fluff with a fork. Add the vinegar and mirin, then stir to combine well.
- Finish and Serve
- Divide the quinoa evenly among 4 mason jars or single-serving containers. Let it cool before sealing the lids.

Nutrition Info: Calories: 192 Cal ;Fat: 3 g :Carbs: 35 g ;Protein: 6 g ;Fiber: 3 g

Loaded Baked Potatoes

Servings: 2

Cooking Time: 32 Minutes

Ingredients:

- 1/2 cup cooked chickpeas
- 2 medium potatoes, scrubbed
- 1 cup broccoli florets, steamed
- 1/4 cup vegan bacon bits
- 2 tablespoons all-purpose seasoning
- ¼ cup vegan cheese sauce
- 1/2 cup vegan sour cream

Directions:

1. Pierce hole in the potatoes, microwave them for minutes over high heat setting until soft to touch, and then bake them for 20 minutes at 450 degrees F until very tender.
2. Open the potatoes, mash the flesh with a fork, then top evenly with remaining ingredients and serve.

Nutrition Info: Calories: 422 Cal ;Fat: 16 g :Carbs: 59 g ;Protein: 9 g ;Fiber: 6 g

Pesto With Squash Ribbons And Fettuccine

Servings: 4

Cooking Time: 0 Minute

Ingredients:

- For the Pesto
- 1/3 cup pumpkin seeds, toasted
- 1 cup cilantro leaves
- 2 teaspoons chopped jalapeño, deseeded
- 1 teaspoon minced garlic
- 1 lime, juiced
- ½ teaspoon of sea salt
- ⅓ cup olive oil
- For Pasta and Squash Ribbons
- 8 ounces fettuccine, whole-grain, cooked
- 2 small zucchini
- 1 yellow squash

Directions:

- Prepare ribbons, and for this, slice zucchini and squash by using a vegetable peeler and then set aside until required.

1. Prepare pesto, and for this, place all its ingredients in a food processor and pulse for minutes until blended.
2. Place vegetable ribbons in a bowl, add cooked pasta, then add prepared pesto and toss until well coated.
3. Serve straight away.

Nutrition Info: Calories: 351 Cal ;Fat: 20 g :Carbs: 38.8 g ;Protein: 8 g ;Fiber: 6.1 g

Sautéed Cremini Mushrooms

Servings: 4

Cooking Time: 10 Minutes

Ingredients:

- 4 tablespoons olive oil
- 4 tablespoons shallots, chopped
- 2 cloves garlic, minced
- 1 ½ pounds Cremini mushrooms, sliced
- 1/4 cup dry white wine
- Sea salt and ground black pepper, to taste

Directions:

1. In a sauté pan, heat the olive oil over a moderately high heat.
2. Now, sauté the shallot for 3 to 4 minutes or until tender and translucent. Add in the garlic and continue to cook for 30 seconds more or until aromatic.
3. Stir in the Cremini mushrooms, wine, salt and black pepper; continue sautéing an additional 6 minutes, until your mushrooms are lightly browned. Bon appétit!

Nutrition Info: Per Serving: Calories: 197; Fat: 15.5g; Carbs: 8.8g; Protein: 7.3g

Garlic And Herb Mushroom Skillet

Servings: 4

Cooking Time: 10 Minutes

Ingredients:

- 4 tablespoons vegan butter
- 1 ½ pounds oyster mushrooms halved
- 3 cloves garlic, minced
- 1 teaspoon dried oregano
- 1 teaspoon dried rosemary
- 1 teaspoon dried parsley flakes
- 1 teaspoon dried marjoram
- 1/2 cup dry white wine
- Kosher salt and ground black pepper, to taste

Directions:

- In a sauté pan, heat the olive oil over a moderately high heat.
- Now, sauté the mushrooms for 3 minutes or until they release the liquid. Add in the garlic and continue to cook for 30 seconds more or until aromatic.
- Stir in the spices and continue sautéing an additional 6 minutes, until your mushrooms are lightly browned.

- Bon appétit!

Nutrition Info: Per Serving: Calories: 207; Fat: 15.2g; Carbs: 12.7g; Protein: 9.1g

Keto Cauliflower Rice

Servings: 5

Cooking Time: 10 Minutes

Ingredients:

- 2 medium heads cauliflower, stems and leaves removed, 4 tablespoons extra-virgin olive oil
- 4 garlic cloves, pressed
- 1/2 teaspoon red pepper flakes, crushed
- Sea salt and ground black pepper, to taste
- 1/4 cup flat-leaf parsley, roughly chopped

Directions:

1. Pulse the cauliflower in a food processor with the S-blade until they're broken into "rice".
2. Heat the olive oil in a saucepan over medium-high heat. Once hot, cook the garlic until fragrant or about 1 minute.
3. Add in the cauliflower rice, red pepper, salt and black pepper and continue sautéing for a further 7 to 8 minutes.
4. Taste adjust the seasonings and garnish with fresh parsley. Bon appétit!

Nutrition Info: Per Serving: Calories: 135; Fat: 11.5g; Carbs: 7.2g; Protein: 2.4g

Roasted Rosemary Potatoes

Servings: 4

Cooking Time: 30 Minutes

Ingredients:

- 1½ pounds baby red potatoes, halved
- 2 tablespoons extra-virgin olive oil
- 3 garlic cloves, minced
- 1 tablespoon minced fresh rosemary
- ¾ teaspoon sea salt

Directions:

- Preparing the Ingredients.
- Preheat the oven to 4°F. Line a baking sheet with parchment paper.
- In a large bowl, toss the potatoes with the oil, garlic, rosemary, and salt until well combined.
- Bake
- Spread the potatoes evenly on the prepared baking sheet and bake for 1minutes. Toss with a spatula and bake for an additional 15 minutes, or until golden brown.

Nutrition Info: Calories: 167 Cal ;Fat: 9 g :Carbs: 11 g ;Protein: 4 g ;Fiber: 0 g

Lentil Meatballs With Coconut Curry Sauce

Servings: 14

Cooking Time: 60 Minutes

Ingredients:

- For the Lentil Meatballs:
- 6 ounces tofu, firm, drained
- 1 cup black lentils
- ½ cup quinoa
- 1 teaspoon garlic powder
- 1 teaspoon salt
- 1/3 cup chopped cilantro
- 1 teaspoon fennel seed
- 1 Tablespoon olive oil
- For the Curry:
- 1 large tomato, diced
- 2 teaspoons minced garlic
- 1 tablespoon grated ginger
- 1 teaspoon brown sugar
- ½ teaspoon ground turmeric
- ¼ teaspoon cayenne pepper
- ½ teaspoon salt
- ¼ teaspoon ground black pepper

- 1 tablespoon lime juice
- 2 tablespoons olive oil
- 1 tablespoon dried fenugreek leaves
- 13.5 ounces coconut milk, unsweetened

Directions:

- Boil lentils and fennel in 3 cups water over high heat, then simmer for 25 minutes, and when done, drain them and set aside until required.
- Meanwhile, boil the quinoa in 1 cup water over high heat and then simmer for 15 minutes over low heat until cooked.
- Prepare the sauce and for this, place a pot over medium heat, add oil, ginger, and garlic, cook for 2 minutes, then stir in turmeric, cook for 1 minute, add tomatoes and cook for 5 minutes.
- Add remaining ingredients for the sauce, stir until mixed and simmer until ready to serve.
- Transfer half of the lentils in a food processor, add quinoa and pulse until the mixture resembles sand.
- Tip the mixture into a bowl, add remaining ingredients for the meatballs and stir until well mixed.

- Place tofu in a food processor, add 1 tablespoon oil, process until the smooth paste comes together, add to lentil mixture, stir until well mixed and shape the mixture into small balls.
- Place the balls on a baking sheet, spray with oil and bake for 20 minutes until golden brown.
- Add balls into the warm sauce, toss until coated, sprinkle with cilantro, and serve.

Nutrition Info: Calories: 150.8 Cal ;Fat: 4.6 g :Carbs: 18 g ;Protein: 10.2 g ;Fiber: 6.8 g

Stuffed Eggplant Rolls

Servings: 4

Cooking Time: 45 Minutes

Ingredients:

- 1 large or 2 medium eggplants
- Salt and freshly ground black pepper
- 1 tablespoon extra-virgin olive oil
- 2 garlic cloves, minced
- 2 green onions, chopped
- ¼cup ground pine nuts
- 2 tablespoons finely chopped oil-packed sun-dried tomatoes
- 3 tablespoons golden raisins
- 3 tablespoons vegan Parmesan
- 1 tablespoon minced fresh parsley
- 2 cups marinara sauce

Directions:

- Preparing the Ingredients
- Preheat the oven to 375°F.
- Lightly oil a large baking sheet and a 9 x 1inch baking pan and set side. Cut the eggplants lengthwise into ¼-inch-thick slices and arrange them on the prepared baking sheet. Bake until

partially softened for about 15 minutes. Remove from the oven, sprinkle with salt and pepper, and set aside to cool.

- In a large skillet, heat the oil over medium heat. Add the garlic, green onions, and pine nuts and cook while stirring for 1 minute. Stir in the tomatoes, raisins, Parmesan, parsley, and salt and pepper. Mix well. Taste and adjust seasonings if necessary.
- Spread about 2 tablespoons of the stuffing mixture onto each of the softened eggplant slices and roll up the eggplant. Arrange the eggplant bundles, seam side down, in the prepared baking pan.
- Top with the marinara sauce, cover tightly with foil, and bake until tender and hot for about 30 minutes. Serve immediately.

Nutrition Info: Calories: 98 Cal ;Fat: 3.5 g :Carbs: 16 g ;Protein: 8 g ;Fiber 4.3 g

Mushroom And Broccoli Noodles

Servings: 4

Cooking Time: 10 Minutes

Ingredients:

- 2 linguine pasta, whole-grain, cooked
- 8 ounces chestnut mushroom, sliced
- 4 spring onions, sliced
- 1 small head of broccoli, cut into florets, steamed
- ½ teaspoon minced garlic
- ½ teaspoon red chili flakes
- 1 tablespoon sesame oil
- 2 teaspoons hoisin sauce
- ¼ cup roasted cashew
- 3 tablespoons stock

Directions:

- Take a large frying pan, place it over medium heat, add oil and when hot, add mushrooms and cook for 2 minutes until golden.
- Stir in garlic, onion and chili flakes, cook for 1 minute, stir in broccoli and toss in pasta until hot.
- Drizzle with hoisin sauce and tablespoons of stock, toss until mixed, cook for 1 minute and remove the pan from heat.

- Top with cashews, drizzle with some more sesame oil and serve.

Nutrition Info: Calories: 624 Cal ;Fat: 14 g :Carbs: 105 g ;Protein: 25 g ;Fiber: 8 g

Rosemary Beet Chips

Servings: 3

Cooking Time: 20 Minutes

Ingredients:

- 3 large beets, scrubbed, thinly sliced
- 1/8 teaspoon ground black pepper
- ¼ teaspoon of sea salt
- 3 sprigs of rosemary, leaves chopped
- 4 tablespoons olive oil

Directions:

- Spread beet slices in a single layer between two large baking sheets, brush the slices with oil, then season with spices and rosemary, toss until well coated, and bake for 20 minutes at 375 degrees F until crispy, turning halfway.
- When done, let the chips cool for 10 minutes and then serve.

Nutrition Info: Calories: 79 Cal ;Fat: 4.7 g :Carbs: 8.6 g ;Protein: 1.5 g ;Fiber: 2.5 g

Roasted Cauliflower Tacos

Servings: 8

Cooking Time: 30 Minutes

Ingredients:

FOR THE ROASTED CAULIFLOWER

- 1 head cauliflower, cut into bite-size pieces
- 1 tablespoon extra-virgin olive oil (optional)
- 2 tablespoons whole-wheat flour
- 2 tablespoons nutritional yeast
- 1 to 2 teaspoons smoked paprika
- ½ to 1 teaspoon chili powder
- Pinch sea salt

FOR THE TACOS

- 2 cups shredded lettuce
- 2 cups cherry tomatoes, quartered
- 2 carrots, scrubbed or peeled, and grated
- ½ cup Fresh Mango Salsa
- ½ cup Guacamole
- 8 small whole-grain or corn tortillas
- 1 lime, cut into 8 wedges

Directions:

TO MAKE THE ROASTED CAULIFLOWER

- Preheat the oven to 350°F. Lightly grease a large rectangular baking sheet with olive oil, or line it with parchment paper. In a large bowl, toss the cauliflower pieces with oil (if using), or just rinse them so they're wet. The idea is to get the seasonings to stick. In a smaller bowl, mix together the flour, nutritional yeast, paprika, chili powder, and salt.
- Add the seasonings to the cauliflower, and mix it around with your hands to thoroughly coat. Spread the cauliflower on the baking sheet, and roast for 20 to minutes, or until softened.
- TO MAKE THE TACOS. Prep the veggies, salsa, and guacamole while the cauliflower is roasting. Once the cauliflower is cooked, heat the tortillas for just a few minutes in the oven or in a small skillet. Set everything out on the table, and assemble your tacos as you go. Give a squeeze of fresh lime just before eating.

Nutrition Info: Per Serving: (1 taco) Calories: 198; Total fat: 6g; Carbs: 32g; Fiber: 6g; Protein: 7g

Burrito-stuffed Sweet Potatoes

Servings: 4

Cooking Time: 45 Minutes

Ingredients:

- For Sweet Potatoes:
- 1 cup cooked black beans
- 4 small sweet potatoes
- ½ cup of brown rice
- ½ teaspoon minced garlic
- 1 teaspoon tomato paste
- 1 teaspoon ground cumin
- ¼ teaspoon salt
- ½ teaspoon olive oil
- 1 ¼ cup water
- For the Salsa:
- 1 cup cherry tomatoes, halved
- 1 medium red bell pepper, deseeded, chopped
- ¾ cup chopped red onion
- 2 tablespoon chopped cilantro leaves
- ½ teaspoon salt
- ¼ teaspoon ground black pepper
- 1 ½ teaspoon olive oil
- 1 tablespoon lime juice

- For the Guacamole:
- 1 medium avocado, pitted, peeled
- ½ teaspoon minced garlic
- 2 tablespoons chopped cilantro leaves
- ¼ teaspoon salt
- 1 tablespoon lime juice
- For Serving:
- Shredded cabbage as needed

Directions:

- Prepare sweet potatoes and for this, place them in a baking dish, prick them with a fork and bake for 45 minutes at 400 degrees F until very tender.
- Meanwhile, place a medium saucepan over medium heat, add rice and beans, stir in salt, oil, and tomatoes paste, pour in water and bring the mixture to boil.
- Switch heat to medium-low level, simmer for 40 minutes until all the liquid has absorbed and set aside until required.
- Prepare the salsa and for this, place all its ingredients in a bowl and stir until combined, set aside until required.
- Prepare the guacamole and for this, place the avocado in a bowl, mash well, then add remaining

ingredients, stir until combined, and set aside until required.

- When sweet potatoes are baked, cut them along the top, pull back the skin, then split and top with rice and beans mixture.
- Top with salsa and guacamole and cabbage and serve.

Nutrition Info: Calories: 388 Cal ;Fat: 11 g :Carbs: 67.1 g ;Protein: 10.5 g ;Fiber: 15.7 g

Edamame Donburi

Servings: 4

Cooking Time: 20 Minutes

Ingredients:

- 1 cup fresh or frozen shelled edamame
- 1 tablespoon canola or grapeseed oil
- 1 medium yellow onion, minced
- 5 shiitake mushroom caps, lightly rinsed, patted dry, and cut into 1/4-inch strips
- 1 teaspoon grated fresh ginger
- 3 green onions, minced
- 8 ounces firm tofu, drained and crumbled
- 2 tablespoons soy sauce
- 3 cups hot cooked white or brown rice
- 1 tablespoon toasted sesame oil
- 1 tablespoon toasted sesame seeds, for garnish

Directions:

- Preparing the Ingredients
- In a small saucepan of boiling salted water, cook the edamame until tender, about 10 minutes. Drain and set aside.
- In a large skillet, heat the canola oil over medium heat. Add the onion, cover, and cook until

softened, about 5 minutes. Add the mushrooms and cook, uncovered, 5 minutes longer. Stir in the ginger and green onions. Add the tofu and soy sauce and cook until heated through, stirring to combine well, about 5 minutes. Stir in the cooked edamame and cook until heated through, about 5 minutes.

- Finish and Serve
- Divide the hot rice among 4 bowls, top each with the edamame and tofu mixture, and drizzle on the sesame oil. Sprinkle with sesame seeds and serve immediately.

Nutrition Info: Calories: 100.8 Cal ;Fat: 4.6 g :Carbs: 8 g ;Protein: 7.3g ;Fiber: 3.4 g

Roasted Cauliflower With Herbs

Servings: 4

Cooking Time: 30 Minutes

Ingredients:

- 1 ½ pounds cauliflower florets
- 1/4 cup olive oil, 4 cloves garlic, whole
- 1 tablespoon fresh basil
- 1 tablespoon fresh coriander
- 1 tablespoon fresh oregano, 1 tablespoon fresh rosemary, 1 tablespoon fresh parsley
- Sea salt and ground black pepper, to taste
- 1 teaspoon red pepper flakes

Directions:

- Begin by preheating the oven to 425 degrees F. Toss the cauliflower with the olive oil and arrange them on a parchment-lined roasting pan.
- Then, roast the cauliflower florets for about minutes; toss them with the garlic and spices and continue cooking an additional 10 minutes.
- Serve warm. Bon appétit!

Nutrition Info: Per Serving: Calories: 175; Fat: 14g; Carbs: 10.7g; Protein: 3.7g

Stuffed Peppers With Kidney Beans

Servings: 4

Cooking Time: 35 Minutes

Ingredients:

- 3.5 ounces cooked kidney beans
- 1 big tomato, diced
- 3.5 ounces sweet corn, canned
- 2 medium bell peppers, deseeded, halved
- ½ of medium red onion, peeled, diced
- 1 teaspoon garlic powder
- 1/3 teaspoon ground black pepper
- 2/3 teaspoon salt
- ½ teaspoon dried basil
- 3 teaspoons parsley
- ½ teaspoon dried thyme
- 3 tablespoons cashew
- 1 teaspoon olive oil

Directions:

- Switch on the oven, then set it to 400 degrees F and let it preheat.
- Take a large skillet pan, place it over medium heat, add oil and when hot, add onion and cook for minutes until translucent.

- Add beans, tomatoes, and corn, stir in garlic and cashews and cook for 5 minutes.
- Stir in salt, black pepper, parsley, basil, and thyme, remove the pan from heat and evenly divide the mixture between bell peppers.
- Bake the peppers for 2minutes until tender, then top with parsley and serve.

Nutrition Info: Calories: 139 Cal ;Fat: 1.6 g :Carbs: 18 g ;Protein: 5.1 g ;Fiber: 3.3 g

Zucchini Hummus

Servings: 8

Cooking Time: 0 Minute

Ingredients:

- 1 cup diced zucchini
- 1/2 teaspoon sea salt
- 1 teaspoon minced garlic
- 2 teaspoons ground cumin
- 3 tablespoons lemon juice
- 1/3 cup tahini

Directions:

- Place all the ingredients in a food processor and pulse for 2 minutes until smooth.
- Tip the hummus in a bowl, drizzle with oil and serve.

Nutrition Info: Calories: 65 Cal ;Fat: 5 g :Carbs: 3 g ;Protein: 2 g ;Fiber: 1 g

Ratatouille

Servings: 4

Cooking Time: 15 Minutes

Ingredients:

- 2 medium zucchini, sliced into ½-inch sliced moons
- 1 large eggplant, cut into ½-inch pieces
- 2 medium tomatoes, cut into ¾-inch wedges
- 1 red bell pepper, sliced into ½-inch strips
- 1 medium white onion, sliced
- 12 cloves of garlic, peeled
- 1 teaspoon salt
- 1 teaspoon balsamic vinegar
- 1/3 teaspoon ground black pepper
- 3 tablespoons rosemary and thyme
- Olive oil as needed

Directions:

- Prepare all the vegetables, then spread them in a single layer on a greased sheet pan, add garlic and herbs, drizzle with oil, toss until coated and season with salt with black pepper.
- Toss the vegetables, roast them for 40 minutes at 400 degrees F, tossing halfway, and then continue

roasting for minutes at 300 degrees F until tender.

- When done, taste to adjust salt, drizzle with vinegar and serve.

Nutrition Info: Calories: 147 Cal ;Fat: 9.7 g :Carbs: 15.1 g ;Protein: 2.5 g ;Fiber: 4.2 g

Easy Roasted Kohlrabi

Servings: 4

Cooking Time: 30 Minutes

Ingredients:

- 1 pound kohlrabi bulbs, peeled and sliced
- 4 tablespoons olive oil
- 1/2 teaspoon mustard seeds
- 1 teaspoon celery seeds, 1 teaspoon dried marjoram,1 teaspoon granulated garlic, minced
- Sea salt and ground black pepper, to taste
- 2 tablespoons nutritional yeast

Directions:

- Start by preheating your oven to 450 degrees F.
- Toss the kohlrabi with the olive oil and spices until well coated. Arrange the kohlrabi in a single layer on a parchment-lined roasting pan.
- Bake the kohlrabi in the preheated oven for about 15 minutes; stir them and continue to cook an additional 15 minutes.
- Sprinkle nutritional yeast over the warm kohlrabi and serve immediately. Bon appétit!

Nutrition Info: Per Serving: Calories: 177; Fat: 14g; Carbs: 10.5g; Protein: 4.5g

Mediterranean-style Green Beans

Servings: 4

Cooking Time: 20 Minutes

Ingredients:

- 2 tablespoons olive oil
- 1 red bell pepper, seeded and diced
- 1 ½ pounds green beans
- 4 garlic cloves, minced
- 1/2 teaspoon mustard seeds
- 1/2 teaspoon fennel seeds
- 1 teaspoon dried dill weed
- 2 tomatoes, pureed
- 1 cup cream of celery soup
- 1 teaspoon Italian herb mix
- 1 teaspoon cayenne pepper
- Salt and freshly ground black pepper

Directions:

- Heat the olive oil in a saucepan over medium flame. Once hot, fry the peppers and green beans for about 5 minutes, stirring periodically to promote even cooking.

- Add in the garlic, mustard seeds, fennel seeds and dill and continue sautéing an additional 1 minute or until fragrant.
- Add in the pureed tomatoes, cream of celery soup, Italian herb mix, cayenne pepper, salt and black pepper. Continue to simmer, covered, for about 9 minutes or until the green beans are tender.
- Taste, adjust the seasonings and serve warm. Bon appétit!

Nutrition Info: Per Serving: Calories: 159; Fat: 8.8g; Carbs: 18.8g; Protein: 4.8g

Spaghetti Squash Primavera

Servings: 4

Cooking Time: 40 Minutes

Ingredients:

- 1 large spaghetti squash (roughly 4 pounds), halved and seeded
- 3 tablespoons extra-virgin olive oil, divided
- 1 onion, chopped
- 2 cups chopped broccoli florets
- ½ cup pitted and sliced green olives
- 1 cup halved cherry tomatoes
- 3 garlic cloves, minced
- 1½ teaspoons Italian seasoning
- ¾ teaspoon sea salt
- ½ teaspoon black pepper
- Pine nuts, for garnish (optional)
- Walnut Parmesan or store-bought vegan Parmesan, for garnish (optional)
- Red pepper flakes, for garnish (optional)

Directions:

- Preparing the Ingredients.
- Preheat the oven to 400°F.
- Line a baking sheet with parchment paper.

- Brush the rims and the insides of both squash halves with 1 tablespoon of olive oil. Place on the prepared baking sheet, cut-sides down.
- Bake for 35-45 minutes, until a fork can easily pierce the flesh. Set aside until cool enough to handle for 10-15 minutes.
- While the squash is cooling, heat 1 tablespoon of olive oil in a large skillet over medium heat.
- Add the onion and broccoli and sauté for 3 minutes, or until the onion is soft. Add the olives and tomatoes and cook for an additional 3-5 minutes, or until the broccoli is fork-tender and the tomatoes have started to wilt. Add the garlic and cook for 1 additional minute, or until fragrant.
- Finish and Serve
    - Remove from the heat. Use a fork to gently pull the squash flesh from the skin and separate the flesh into strands. The strands wrap around the squash horizontally, so rake your fork in the same direction as the strands to make the longest spaghetti squash noodles. Toss the noodles into the skillet with the vegetables. Add 1 tablespoon of olive oil, Italian seasoning,

salt and pepper and mix well to combine. Divide among bowls and garnish with pine nuts, Parmesan, and red pepper flakes if desired.

Nutrition Info: Calories: 190.8 Cal ;Fat: 6.6 g :Carbs: 21 g ;Protein: 7.2 g ;Fiber: 4.8 g

Mango Cabbage Wraps

Servings: 4

Cooking Time: 35 Minutes

Ingredients:

- 2 tablespoons chopped peanuts, toasted
- 1 small head of green cabbage
- 2 tablespoons coconut flakes, unsweetened, toasted
- For the Baked Tofu:
- 15 ounces tofu, extra-firm, drained, cut into ½-inch cubed
- 2 teaspoons cornstarch
- 1 tablespoon soy sauce
- 1 tablespoon olive oil
- For the Peanut Sauce:
- 1 teaspoon minced garlic
- 2 tablespoons soy sauce
- 2 tablespoons apple cider vinegar
- 4 tablespoons lime juice
- 2 tablespoons honey
- 1/3 cup peanut butter
- 2 teaspoons toasted sesame oil
- For the Mango Pico:

- 4 green onions, chopped
- 2 mangos, peeled, stoned, diced
- 1 medium red bell pepper, cored, chopped
- 1 jalapeño, minced
- 1/3 cup cilantro leaves, chopped
- ¼ teaspoon salt
- 2 tablespoons lime juice

Directions:

- Prepare tofu and for this, place tofu pieces on a baking sheet, drizzle with tablespoon oil and soy sauce, and toss until coated.
- Sprinkle with 1 teaspoon cornstarch, toss until incorporated, sprinkle with remaining corn starch, toss until well coated, arrange tofu pieces in a single layer and bake for 35 minutes at 400 degrees F until crispy and golden brown.
- Meanwhile, prepare the peanut sauce and for this, place all its ingredients in a food processor and pulse for 2 minutes until blended, set aside until required.
- Prepare the salsa and for this, place all its ingredients in a bowl and toss until mixed.

- When tofu has baked, take a pan, place it over medium heat, add toast peanuts and coconut flakes in it, and then add tofu pieces.
- Pour in two-third of the peanut sauce, toss until well coated, cook for 5 minutes until its edges begin to bowl, then transfer tofu to a plate and let cool for 10 minutes.
- Prepare the wrap and for this, pull out one leaf at a time from the cabbage, add some salsa, top with tofu, drizzle with remaining peanut sauce and serve.

Nutrition Info: Calories: 448 Cal ;Fat: 26 g :Carbs: 40 g ;Protein: 20 g ;Fiber: 6.6 g

Sautéed Zucchini With Herbs

Servings: 4

Cooking Time: 10 Minutes

Ingredients:

- 2 tablespoons olive oil
- 1 onion, sliced, 2 garlic cloves, minced
- 1 ½ pounds zucchini, sliced
- Sea salt and fresh ground black pepper, to taste
- 1 teaspoon cayenne pepper
- 1/2 teaspoon dried basil
- 1/2 teaspoon dried oregano
- 1/2 teaspoon dried rosemary

Directions:

- In a saucepan, heat the olive oil over medium-high heat.
- Once hot, sauté the onion for about 3 minutes or until tender. Then, sauté the garlic for about 1 minute until aromatic.
- Add in the zucchini, along with the spices and continue to sauté for 6 minutes more until tender.
- Taste and adjust the seasonings. Bon appétit!

Nutrition Info: Per Serving: Calories: 99; Fat: 7.4g; Carbs: 6g; Protein: 4.3g

Sauces & Condiments Recipes

Tomato Sauce

Servings: 6

Cooking Time: 4 Hours 20 Minutes

Ingredients:

- 10 ripe tomatoes
- 3 tablespoons olive oil
- 2 carrots, peeled and chopped
- 1 green bell pepper, seeded and chopped
- 1 yellow onion, chopped
- 4 garlic cloves, minced
- 1 bay leaf
- 2 celery stalks, halved
- ¼ cup fresh basil, chopped
- 3 tablespoons homemade vegetable broth
- 2 tablespoons balsamic vinegar
- ¼ teaspoon Italian seasoning
- 2 tablespoons tomato paste

Directions:

- In a pan of boiling water, add tomatoes and cook for about minute.
- Drain well and transfer into a bowl of ice water.
- Let them cool. Remove the peel and seeds of the tomatoes.
- Chop 2 tomatoes and set aside.
- In a blender, add the remaining 8 tomatoes and pulse until a puree forms.
- In a large pan, heat the oil over medium heat and sauté the carrots, celery, bell pepper, onion, and garlic, for about 5 minutes.
- Add chopped tomatoes, tomato puree, and remaining all ingredients (except tomato paste) and bring to a boil.
- Lower the heat to low and simmer for about 2 hours, stirring occasionally.
- Stir in the tomato paste and simmer for about 2 hours more.
- Discard the celery and bay leaf set aside to cool completely before serving.

Nutrition Info: Calories: 98.8 Cal ;Fat: 3.6 g :Carbs: 8 g ;Protein: 2.2 g ;Fiber: 3.8 g

Vegan Bean Pesto

Servings: 2

Cooking Time: 5 Minutes

Ingredients:

- 1 can (15 oz.) white beans, drained, rinsed
- 2 cups basil leaves, washed, dried
- ½ cup non-dairy milk
- 2 tablespoons olive oil
- 3 tablespoons nutritional yeast
- 1 garlic clove, peeled
- Pepper and salt to taste

Directions:

- Blend all the ingredients (except the seasonings) in a blender until smooth.
- Sprinkle with pepper and salt to taste, then blend for 1 extra minute. Enjoy with pasta.

Kale And Hemp Seed Pesto

Servings: 10

Cooking Time: 10 Minutes

Ingredients:

- 1/2 cup hemp seeds, hulled
- 1/2 cup raw cashews
- 2 cloves garlic, minced
- 1 cup fresh kale, 1/2 cup fresh basil
- 1/2 cup fresh parsley
- 3 tablespoons nutritional yeast
- 1 tablespoon fresh lemon juice, 1 teaspoon sherry vinegar, Sea salt and ground black pepper, to taste
- 1/4 cup olive oil

Directions:

- In your food processor, place all ingredients, except for the oil. Process until well combined.
- While the machine is running, gradually pour in the olive oil until the sauce is uniform and creamy. Serve with pasta, crackers or breadsticks. Bon appétit!

Nutrition Info: Per Serving: Calories: 110; Fat: 8.9g; Carbs: 8.5g; Protein: 4g

Nice Spiced Cherry Cider

Servings: 16

Cooking Time: 3 Hours

Ingredients:

- 2 cinnamon sticks, each about 3 inches long
- 6-ounce of cherry gelatin
- 4 quarts of apple cider

Directions:

- Using a 6-quarts slow cooker, pour the apple cider and add the cinnamon stick.
- Stir, then cover the slow cooker with its lid. Plug in the cooker and let it cook for 3 hours at the high heat setting or until it is heated thoroughly.
- Then add and stir the gelatin properly, then continue cooking for another hour.
- When done, remove the cinnamon sticks and serve the drink hot or cold.
- **Nutrition Info: Calories: 70 Cal ;Fat: 3.6 g :Carbs: 5 g ;Protein: 1.2 g ;Fiber: 3.8 g**

Homemade Guacamole

Servings: 7

Cooking Time: 10 Minutes

Ingredients:

- 2 avocados, peeled, pitted
- 1 lemon, juiced
- Sea salt and ground black pepper, to taste
- 1 small onion, diced
- 2 tablespoons chopped fresh cilantro
- 1 large tomato, diced

Directions:

- Mash the avocados, together with the remaining ingredients in a mixing bowl.
- Place the guacamole in your refrigerator until ready to serve. Bon appétit!

Nutrition Info: Per Serving: Calories: 107; Fat: 8.6g; Carbs: 7.9g; Protein: 1.6g

Garlic Alfredo Sauce

Servings: 4

Cooking Time: 5 Minutes

Ingredients:

- 1 1/2 cups cashews, unsalted , soaked in warm water for 15 minutes
- 6 cloves of garlic, peeled, minced
- 1/2 medium sweet onion, peeled, chopped
- 1 teaspoon salt
- 1/4 cup nutritional yeast
- 1 tablespoon lemon juice
- 2 tablespoons olive oil
- 2 cups almond milk, unsweetened
- 12 ounces fettuccine pasta, cooked, for serving

Directions:

- Take a small saucepan, place it over medium heat, add oil and when hot, add onion and garlic, and cook for 5 minutes until sauté.
- Meanwhile, drain the cashews, transfer them into a food processor, add remaining ingredients including onion mixture, except for pasta, and pulse for 3 minutes until very smooth.

- Pour the prepared sauce over pasta, toss until coated and serve.

Nutrition Info: Calories: 439 Cal ;Fat: 20 g :Carbs: 52 g ;Protein: 15 g ;Fiber: 4 g

Tomato Sauce With Garlic And Herbs

Servings: 12

Cooking Time: 25 Minutes

Ingredients:

- 3 tablespoons olive oil
- 4 garlic cloves, minced
- 1 teaspoon dried parsley flakes
- 1 teaspoon dried rosemary
- 1 teaspoon dried basil
- Kosher salt and black pepper, to taste
- 1 teaspoon red pepper flakes, crushed
- 1 (28-ounce can tomatoes, crushed

Directions:

- In a medium saucepan, heat the olive oil over a moderately high heat. Sauté the garlic for minute or until aromatic.
- Add in the herbs, spices and tomatoes and turn the heat to a simmer. Continue to simmer for about minutes.
- Bon appétit!

Nutrition Info: Per Serving: Calories: 44; Fat: 3.5g; Carbs: 3.1g; Protein: 0.7g

Favorite Cranberry Sauce

Servings: 8

Cooking Time: 15 Minutes

Ingredients:

- 1/2 cup brown sugar
- 1/2 cup water
- 8 ounces cranberries, fresh or frozen
- A pinch of allspice
- A pinch of sea salt
- 1 tablespoon crystallized ginger

Directions:

- In a heavy-bottomed saucepan, bring the sugar and water to a rolling boil.
- Stir until the sugar has dissolved.
- Add in the cranberries, followed by the remaining ingredients. Turn the heat to a simmer and continue to cook for 10 to 12 minutes or until the cranberries burst.
- Let it cool at room temperature. Store in a glass jar in your refrigerator. Bon appétit!

Nutrition Info: Per Serving: Calories: 62; Fat: 0.6g; Carbs: 16g; Protein: 0.2g

Classic Velouté Sauce

Servings: 5

Cooking Time: 10 Minutes

Ingredients:

- 2 tablespoons vegan butter
- 2 tablespoons all-purpose flour
- 1 ½ cups vegetable stock
- 1/4 teaspoon white pepper

Directions:

- Melt the vegan butter in a saucepan over a moderate flame. Add in the flour and continue to cook, whisking continuously to avoid lumps.
- Gradually and slowly pour in the vegetable stock and continue whisking for about 5 minutes until the sauce has thickened.
- Add in white pepper and stir to combine well. Bon appétit!

Nutrition Info: Per Serving: Calories: 65; Fat: 5.2g; Carbs: 2.4g; Protein: 1.9g

Pistachio Dip

Servings: 8

Cooking Time: 0 Minute

Ingredients:

- 2 tbsp. lemon juice
- 1 t. extra virgin olive oil
- 2 tbsp. of the following:
- tahini
- parsley, chopped
- 2 cloves of garlic
- ½ c. pistachios shelled
- 15 oz. garbanzo beans, save the liquid from the can
- Salt and pepper to taste

Directions:

- Using a food processor, add pistachios, pepper, sea salt, lemon juice, olive oil, tahini, parsley, garlic, and garbanzo beans. Pulse until mixed.
- Using the liquid from the garbanzo beans, add to the dip while slowly blending until it reaches your desired consistency.
- **Nutrition Info: Per Serving: Calories: 65; Fat: 5.2g; Carbs: 3.4g; Protein: 1.9g**

Salsa

Servings: 1 To 1 ½ Cups

Cooking Time: 5 Minutes

Ingredients:

- Pinch of salt
- Pinch of black, ground pepper
- 1 tablespoon of extra-virgin olive oil
- ½ tablespoon of lime juice
- 1 clove of garlic, diced
- 1 shallot, diced, 1 cup of cherry tomatoes
- 1 jalapeno pepper, seeds removed and diced
- ¼ cup of cilantro

Directions:

- Add all ingredients into a blender, pulse until coarsely chopped or smooth depending on your preference. Serve while fresh!

Tips:

- Add bell peppers or pineapple for a twist to this delicious salsa recipe.
- For a spicier salsa, leave the jalapeno seeds intact.

Nutrition Info: Per Serving: Calories: 75; Fat: 4.2g; Carbs: 1.4g; Protein: 1 g

Coconut Peanut Butter Fudge

Servings: 20

Cooking Time: 0 Minute

Ingredients:

- 12 oz smooth peanut butter
- 3 tbsp coconut oil
- 4 tbsp coconut cream
- 15 drops liquid stevia
- Pinch of salt

Directions:

- Line baking tray with parchment paper.
- Melt coconut oil in a saucepan over low heat.
- Add peanut butter, coconut cream, stevia, and salt in a saucepan. Stir well.
- Pour fudge mixture into the prepared baking tray and place in refrigerator for 1 hour.
- Cut into pieces and serve.

Nutrition Info: Per Serving: Calories: 65; Fat: 5.2g; Carbs: 2.4g; Protein: 1.9g

Kale And Walnut Pesto

Servings: 4

Cooking Time: 10 Minutes

Ingredients:

- 1/2 bunch kale, leaves chop
- 1/2 cup chopped walnuts
- 2 cloves of garlic, peeled
- 1/4 cup nutritional yeast
- ½ of lemon, juiced
- 1/4 cup olive oil
- ¼ teaspoon. ground black pepper
- 1/3 teaspoon. salt

Directions:

- Place a large pot filled with water over medium heat, bring it to boil, then add kale and boil for 5 minutes until tender.
- Drain kale, then transfer it in a blender, add remaining ingredients and then pulse for 5 minutes until smooth.
- Serve straight away.

Nutrition Info: Calories: 344 Cal ;Fat: 29 g :Carbs: 16 g ;Protein: 9 g ;Fiber: 6 g

Thai-style Coconut Sauce

Servings: 4

Cooking Time: 10 Minutes

Ingredients:

- 1 tablespoon coconut oil
- 1 teaspoon garlic, minced
- 1 teaspoon fresh ginger, minced
- 1 lemon, juiced and zested
- 1 teaspoon turmeric powder
- 1/2 cup coconut milk, 1 tablespoon soy sauce
- 1 teaspoon coconut sugar, or more to taste
- A pinch of salt
- A pinch of grated nutmeg

Directions:

- In a small saucepan, melt the coconut oil over medium heat. Once hot, cook the garlic and ginger for about minute or until aromatic.
- Turn the heat to a simmer and add in the lemon, turmeric, coconut milk, soy sauce, coconut sugar, salt and nutmeg; continue to simmer for 1 minute or until heated through.

Nutrition Info: Per Serving: Calories: 68; Fat: 5.1g; Carbs: 4.7g; Protein: 1.4g

Peanut Butter Shake

Servings: 2

Cooking Time: 5 Minutes

Ingredients:

- 1 cup plant-based milk
- 1 handful kale
- 2 bananas, frozen
- 2 Tbsp peanut butter
- ½ tsp ground cinnamon
- ¼ tsp vanilla powder

Directions:

- Use a blender to combine all the ingredients for your shake.
- Enjoy it!

Nutrition Info: Per Serving: Calories: 65; Fat: 5.2g; Carbs: 2.4g; Protein: 1.9g

Hibiscus Tea

Servings: 2

Cooking Time: 5 Minutes

Ingredients:

- 1 tablespoon of raisins, diced
- 6 Almonds, raw and unsalted
- ½ teaspoon of hibiscus powder
- 2 cups of water

Directions:

- Bring the water to a boil in a small saucepan, add in the hibiscus powder and raisins. Give it a good stir, cover and let simmer for a further two minutes.
- Strain into a teapot and serve with a side helping of almonds.

Tips:

- As an alternative to this tea, do not strain it and serve with the raisin pieces still swirling around in the teacup.
- You could also serve this tea chilled for those hotter days.

- Double or triple the recipe to provide you with iced-tea to enjoy during the week without having to make a fresh pot each time.

Nutrition Info: Per Serving: Calories: 65; Fat: 5.2g; Carbs: 2.4g; Protein: 1.9g

Barbecue Tahini Sauce

Servings: 8

Cooking Time: 0 Minute

Ingredients:

- 6 tablespoons tahini
- 3/4 teaspoon garlic powder
- 1/8 teaspoon red chili powder
- 2 teaspoons maple syrup
- 1/4 teaspoon salt
- 3 teaspoons molasses
- 3 teaspoons apple cider vinegar
- 1/4 teaspoon liquid smoke
- 10 teaspoons tomato paste
- 1/2 cup water

Directions:

- Place all the ingredients in the order in a food processor or blender and then pulse for 3 to 5 minutes at high speed until smooth.
- Tip the sauce in a bowl and then serve.

Nutrition Info: Calories: 86 Cal ;Fat: 5 g :Carbs: 7 g ;Protein: 2 g ;Fiber: 0 g

Strawberry Grapefruit Smoothie

Servings: 2

Cooking Time: 5 Minutes

Ingredients:

- 1 banana
- ½ cup strawberries, frozen
- 1 grapefruit
- ¼ cup milk
- ¼ cup plain yoghurt
- 2 Tbsp honey
- ½ tsp ginger, chopped

Directions:

- Using a mixer, blend all the ingredients.
- When smooth, top your drink with a slice of grapefruit and enjoy it!

Nutrition Info: Per Serving: Calories: 65; Fat: 5.2g; Carbs: 2.4g; Protein: 1.9g

Easiest Vegan Mayo Ever

Servings: 6

Cooking Time: 15 Minutes

Ingredients:

- 1/2 cup olive oil, at room temperature
- 1/4 cup rice milk, unsweetened, at room temperature
- 1 teaspoon yellow mustard
- 1 tablespoon fresh lemon juice
- 1/3 teaspoon kosher salt

Directions:

- Blend the milk, mustard, lemon juice and salt using your high-speed blender.
- While the machine is going, gradually add in the olive oil and continue to blend at a low speed until the mixture has thickened.
- Store in your refrigerator for about 6 days. Bon appétit!

Nutrition Info: Per Serving: Calories: 167; Fat: 18.1g; Carbs: 0.7g; Protein: 0.4g

Vegan Buffalo Sauce

Servings: 1

Cooking Time: 5 Minutes

Ingredients:

- 1/2 cup soy milk
- 1 cup hot sauce
- 1/2 cup vinegar
- 1/2 teaspoon pepper
- 2 tablespoons sugar
- 1/2 teaspoon garlic granules
- 1 tablespoon tomato sauce

Directions:

- Mix soy milk, hot sauce, sugar, vinegar, sugar, pepper, tomato sauce and garlic granules in a pan and cook over medium heat for minutes.
- Let cool and serve.

Nutrition Info: Per Serving: Calories: 65; Fat: 5.2g; Carbs: 2.4g; Protein: 1.9g

Vodka Cream Sauce

Servings: 1

Cooking Time: 5 Minutes

Ingredients:

- 1/4 cup cashews, unsalted , soaked in warm water for 15 minutes
- 24-ounce marinara sauce
- 2 tablespoons vodka
- 1/4 cup water

Directions:

- Drain the cashews, transfer them in a food processor, pour in water, and blend for 2 minutes until smooth.
- Tip the mixture in a pot, stir in pasta sauce and vodka and simmer for 3 minutes over medium heat until done, stirring constantly.
- Serve sauce over pasta.

Nutrition Info: Calories: 207 Cal ;Fat: 16 g :Carbs: 9.2 g ;Protein: 2.4 g ;Fiber: 4.3 g

Cilantro And Parsley Hot Sauce

Servings: 4

Cooking Time: 0 Minute

Ingredients:

- 2 cups of parsley and cilantro leaves with stems
- 4 Thai bird chilies, destemmed, deseeded, torn
- 2 teaspoons minced garlic
- 1 teaspoon salt
- 1/4 teaspoon coriander seed, ground
- 1/4 teaspoon ground black pepper
- 1/2 teaspoon cumin seeds, ground
- 3 green cardamom pods, toasted, ground
- 1/2 cup olive oil

Directions:

- Take a spice blender or a food processor, place all the ingredients in it, and process for 5 minutes until the smooth paste comes together.
- Serve straight away.

Nutrition Info: Calories: 130 Cal ;Fat: 14 g :Carbs: 2 g ;Protein: 1 g ;Fiber: 1 g

Incredible Barbecue Sauce

Servings: 68

Cooking Time: 6 Hours

Ingredients:

- 1/2 cup of chopped white onion
- 1 tablespoon of salt
- 1/4 cup of brown sugar
- 1/2 teaspoon of ground black pepper
- 4 teaspoons of paprika
- 2 tablespoons of molasses
- 1 tablespoon of apple cider vinegar
- 2 tablespoons of Worcestershire sauce
- 1 tablespoon of ground whole-grain mustard paste
- 4 cups of tomato ketchup
- 1/2 cup of water

Directions:

- Using a 6-quarts slow cooker, place all the ingredients except for the salt, cilantro, and stir properly
- Cover it with the lid, plug in the slow cooker and let it cook for 6 hours on the low heat setting or until it is cooked thoroughly.

- When the cooking time is over, with an immersion blender, process the sauce.
- Then continue cooking for 2 hours. While still stirring occasionally.
- Let the sauce cool off completely and serve or store in sterilized jars.

Nutrition Info: Per Serving: Calories: 65; Fat: 5.2g; Carbs: 2.4g; Protein: 1.9g

Ginger Smoothie With Citrus And Mint

Servings: 3

Cooking Time: 3 Minutes

Ingredients:

- 1 head Romaine lettuce, chopped into 4 chunks
- 2 Tbsp hemp seeds
- 5 mandarin oranges, peeled
- 1 banana, frozen
- 1 carrot
- 2-3 mint leaves
- ½ piece ginger root, peeled
- 1 cup water
- ¼ lemon, peeled
- ½ cup ice

Directions:

- Put all the smoothie ingredients in a blender and blend until smooth.
- Enjoy!

Nutrition Info: Per Serving: Calories: 65; Fat: 5.2g; Carbs: 2.4g; Protein: 1.9g

Spicy Red Wine Tomato Sauce

Servings: 4

Cooking Time: 1 Hour

Ingredients:

- 28 ounces puree of whole tomatoes, peeled
- 4 cloves of garlic, peeled
- 1 tablespoon dried basil
- ¼ teaspoon ground black pepper
- 1 tablespoon dried oregano
- ¼ teaspoon red pepper flakes
- 1 tablespoon dried sage
- 1 tablespoon dried thyme
- 3 teaspoon coconut sugar
- 1/2 of lemon, juice
- 1/4 cup red wine

Directions:

- Take a large saucepan, place it over medium heat, add tomatoes and remaining ingredients, stir and simmer for hour or more until thickened and cooked.
- Serve sauce over pasta.

Nutrition Info: Calories: 110 Cal ;Fat: 2.5 g :Carbs: 9 g ;Protein: 2 g ;Fiber: 2 g

Green Goddess Hummus

Servings: 6

Cooking Time: 0 Minute

Ingredients:

- ¼ cup tahini
- ¼ cup lemon juice
- 2 tablespoons olive oil
- ½ cup chopped parsley
- ¼ cup chopped basil
- 3 tablespoons chopped chives
- 1 large clove of garlic, peeled, chopped
- ½ teaspoon salt
- 15-ounce cooked chickpeas
- 2 tablespoons water

Directions:

- Place all the ingredients in the order in a food processor or blender and then pulse for 3 to 5 minutes at high speed until the thick mixture comes together.
- Tip the hummus in a bowl and then serve.

Nutrition Info: Calories: 110.4 Cal ;Fat: 6 g :Carbs: 11.5 g ;Protein: 4.8 g ;Fiber: 2.6 g

Classic Alfredo Sauce

Servings: 4

Cooking Time: 10 Minutes

Ingredients:

- 2 tablespoons olive oil
- 2 cloves garlic, minced
- 2 tablespoons rice flour
- 1 ½ cups rice milk, unsweetened
- Sea salt and ground black pepper, to taste
- 1/2 teaspoon red pepper flakes, crushed
- 4 tablespoons tahini
- 2 tablespoons nutritional yeast

Directions:

- In a large saucepan, heat the olive oil over a moderate heat. Once hot, sauté the garlic for about 30 seconds or until fragrant.
- Add in the rice flour and turn the heat to a simmer. Gradually add in the milk and continue to cook for a few minutes more, whisking constantly to avoid the lumps.
- Add in the salt, black pepper, red pepper flakes, tahini and nutritional yeast.

- Continue to cook on low until the sauce has thickened.
- Store in an airtight container in your refrigerator for up to four days. Bon appétit!

Nutrition Info: Per Serving: Calories: 245; Fat: 17.9g; Carbs: 14.9g; Protein: 8.2g

Authentic French Remoulade

Servings: 9

Cooking Time: 10 Minutes

Ingredients:

- 1 cup vegan mayonnaise
- 1 tablespoon Dijon mustard
- 1 scallion, finely chopped
- 1 teaspoon garlic, minced
- 2 tablespoons capers, coarsely chopped
- 1 tablespoon hot sauce
- 1 tablespoon fresh lemon juice
- 1 tablespoon flat-leaf parsley, chopped

Directions:

- Thoroughly combine all the ingredients in your food processor or blender.
- Blend until uniform and creamy.
- Bon appétit!

Nutrition Info: Per Serving: Calories: 121; Fat: 10.4g; Carbs: 1.3g; Protein: 6.2g

Energizing Ginger Detox Tonic

Servings: 2

Cooking Time: 10 Minutes

Ingredients:

- 1/2 teaspoon of grated ginger, fresh
- 1 small lemon slice ,1/8 teaspoon of cayenne pepper ,1/8 teaspoon of ground turmeric
- 1/8 teaspoon of ground cinnamon
- 1 teaspoon of maple syrup
- 1 teaspoon of apple cider vinegar
- 2 cups of boiling water

Directions:

- Pour the boiling water into a small saucepan, add and stir the ginger, then let it rest for 8 to minutes, before covering the pan.
- Pass the mixture through a strainer and into the liquid, add the cayenne pepper, turmeric, cinnamon and stir properly.
- Add the maple syrup, vinegar, and lemon slice.
- Add and stir an infused lemon and serve immediately.

Nutrition Info: Per Serving: Calories: 65; Fat: 5.2g; Carbs: 2.4g; Protein: 1.9g

Marinara Sauce

Servings: 8

Cooking Time: 22 Minutes

Ingredients:

- 1/3 cup olive oil
- 1 can tomato paste
- 2 cans stewed tomatoes
- ½ cup white wine
- ¼ cup fresh parsley, chopped
- 1 teaspoon dried oregano, crushed
- Salt and ground black pepper, as required
- 1/3 cup olive oil
- 1/3 cup onion, chopped finely
- 1 garlic clove, minced

Directions:

- Add the tomato paste, stewed tomatoes, garlic, parsley and oregano to a blender and blend until smooth.
- Heat oil over medium heat and sauté chopped onions for minutes.
- Add the tomato mixture and wine and cook for about 20 minutes, stirring constantly.
- Remove from the flame and serve when cool.

Nutrition Info: Per Serving: Calories: 65; Fat: 5.2g; Carbs: 2.4g; Protein: 1.9g

Lemon And Rosemary Iced Tea

Servings: 4

Cooking Time: 10 Minutes

Ingredients:

- 4 cups of water
- 4 earl grey tea bags
- ¼ cup of sugar, 2 lemons
- 1 sprig of rosemary

Directions:

- Peel the two lemons and set the fruit aside.
- In a medium saucepan, over medium heat combine the water, sugar, and lemon peels. Bring this to a boil.
- Remove from the heat and place the rosemary and tea into the mixture. Cover the saucepan and steep for five minutes.
- Add the juice of the two peeled lemons to the mixture, strain, chill, and serve.
- Tips:Skip the sugar and use honey to taste.
- Do not squeeze the tea bags as they can cause the tea to become bitter.

Nutrition Info: Per Serving: Calories: 65; Fat: 5.2g; Carbs: 2.4g; Protein: 1.9g

Almond And Sunflower Seed Mayo

Servings: 12

Cooking Time: 10 Minutes

Ingredients:

- 1/4 cup raw sunflower seeds, hulled
- 1/2 cup raw almonds
- 3/4 cup water
- 1/2 teaspoon onion powder
- 1/2 teaspoon garlic powder
- 1/4 teaspoon dried dill
- 1/2 teaspoon sea salt
- 1 cup sunflower seed oil
- 2 tablespoons fresh lime juice
- 1 tablespoon apple cider vinegar

Directions:

- Process all the ingredients, except for the oil, in your blender or food processor until well combined.
- Then, gradually add in the oil and continue to blend at low speed until smooth and creamy.
- Add more spices, if needed.
- Place in your refrigerator until ready to serve. Bon appétit!

Nutrition Info: Per Serving: Calories: 109; Fat: 9.2g; Carbs: 4.4g; Protein: 3.7g

c

lassic Homemade Ketchup

Servings: 10

Cooking Time: 25 Minutes

Ingredients:

- 4 ounces canned tomato paste
- 2 tablespoons agave syrup
- 1/4 cup red wine vinegar
- 1/4 cup water
- 1/2 teaspoon kosher salt
- 1/4 teaspoon garlic powder

Directions:

- Preheat a saucepan over medium flame. Then, add all the ingredients to a saucepan and bring it to a boil.
- Turn the heat to a simmer; let it simmer, stirring continuously, for about minutes or until the sauce has thickened.
- Store in a glass jar in your refrigerator. Bon appétit!

Nutrition Info: Per Serving: Calories: 24; Fat: 0g; Carbs: 5.5g; Protein: 0.5g

Soothing Ginger Tea Drink

Servings: 8

Cooking Time: 2 Hours 20 Minutes

Ingredients:

- 1 tablespoon of minced gingerroot
- 2 tablespoons of honey
- 15 green tea bags
- 32 fluid ounce of white grape juice
- 2 quarts of boiling water

Directions:

- Pour water into a 4-quarts slow cooker, immerse tea bags, cover the cooker and let stand for minutes.
- After 10 minutes, remove and discard tea bags and stir in remaining ingredients.
- Return cover to slow cooker, then plug in and let cook at high heat setting for 2 hours or until heated through.
- When done, strain the liquid and serve hot or cold.

Nutrition Info: Per Serving: Calories: 65; Fat: 5.2g; Carbs: 2.4g; Protein: 1.9g

Herb Avocado Salad Dressing

Servings: 6

Cooking Time: 10 Minutes

Ingredients:

- 1 medium-sized avocado, pitted, peeled and mashed
- 4 tablespoons extra-virgin olive oil
- 4 tablespoons almond milk
- 2 tablespoons cilantro, minced
- 2 tablespoons parsley, minced
- 1 lemon, juiced
- 2 garlic cloves, minced
- 1/2 teaspoon mustard seeds
- 1/2 teaspoon red pepper flakes
- Kosher salt and cayenne pepper, to taste

Directions:

- Mix all the above ingredients in your food processor or blender.
- Blend until uniform, smooth and creamy.
- Bon appétit!

Nutrition Info: Per Serving: Calories: 101; Fat: 9.4g; Carbs: 4.3g; Protein: 1.2g

Brownie Batter Orange Chia Shake

Servings: 2

Cooking Time: 0 Minute

Ingredients:

- 2 tablespoons cocoa powder
- 3 tablespoons chia seeds
- ¼ teaspoon salt
- 4 tablespoons chocolate chips
- 4 teaspoons coconut sugar
- ½ teaspoon orange zest
- ½ teaspoon vanilla extract, unsweetened
- 2 cup almond milk

Directions:

- Place all the ingredients in the order in a food processor or blender and then pulse for 2 to 3 minutes at high speed until smooth.
- Pour the smoothie into two glasses and then serve.

Nutrition Info: Per Serving: Calories: 76; Fat: 4.2g; Carbs: 8.4g; Protein: 1.9g

Vegan Ranch Dressing

Servings: 16

Cooking Time: 0 Minute

Ingredients:

- 1/4 teaspoon. ground black pepper
- 2 teaspoon. chopped parsley
- 1/2 teaspoon. garlic powder
- 1 tablespoon chopped dill
- 1/2 teaspoon. onion powder
- 1 cup vegan mayonnaise
- 1/2 cup soy milk, unsweetened

Directions:

- Take a medium bowl, add all the ingredients in it and then whisk until combined.
- Serve straight away

Nutrition Info: Calories: 16 Cal ;Fat: 9 g :Carbs: 0 g ;Protein: 0 g ;Fiber: 0 g

Barbecue Sauce

Servings: 16

Cooking Time: 0 Minute

Ingredients:

- 8 ounces tomato sauce
- 1 teaspoon garlic powder
- ¼ teaspoon ground black pepper
- 1/2 teaspoon. sea salt
- 2 Tablespoons Dijon mustard
- 3 packets stevia
- 1 teaspoon molasses
- 1 Tablespoon apple cider vinegar
- 2 Tablespoons tamari
- 1 teaspoon liquid aminos

Directions:

- Take a medium bowl, place all the ingredients in it, and stir until combined.
- Serve straight away

Nutrition Info: Calories: 29 Cal ;Fat: 0.1 g :Carbs: 7 g ;Protein: 0.1 g ;Fiber: 0.1 g

Perfect Hollandaise Sauce

Servings: 6

Cooking Time: 15 Minutes

Ingredients:

- 1/2 cup cashews, soaked and drained
- 1 cup almond milk
- 2 tablespoons fresh lemon juice
- 3 tablespoons coconut oil
- 3 tablespoons nutritional yeast
- Sea salt and ground white pepper, to taste
- A pinch of grated nutmeg
- 1/2 teaspoon red pepper flakes, crushed

Directions:

- Puree all the ingredients in a high-speed blender or food processor.
- Then, heat the mixture in a small saucepan over low-medium heat; cook, stirring occasionally, until the sauce has reduced and thickened.
- Bon appétit!

Nutrition Info: Per Serving: Calories: 145; Fat: 12.6g; Carbs: 6.1g; Protein: 3.3g

CPSIA information can be obtained
at www.ICGtesting.com
Printed in the USA
BVHW090254210621
610112BV00002B/42

9 781803 300566